Ethel
KING & M_____
Hereford's Patron Saint

LOGASTON PRESS

FRONT COVER & FRONTISPIECE: Shrine of St Ethelbert, Hereford Cathedral © Gordon Taylor
BACK COVER: St Ethelbert, Stanbury Chapel, Hereford Cathedral © Gordon Taylor

First published in 2018 by Logaston Press
The Holme, Church Road, Eardisley HR3 6NJ, UK
www.logastonpress.co.uk
An imprint of Fircone Books Ltd.

978-1-910839-32-4

Text © Michael Tavinor, 2018; Essay (p. 50) © E.M. Jancey, Ian Bass & Lydia Prosser.
Images © Gordon Taylor, except p. 5 (*coin*) © Canon Sandy Elliott; pp. 20–25 (*Suffolk &
Norfolk churches*) © Simon Knott & Peter Stephens, except p. 21 (*East Wretham*) © John
Salmon [geograph-1701432], p. 21 (*Burnham Sutton*) © Evelyn Simak [geograph-2047689] &
p. 23 (*Falkenham church*) © Adrian S. Pye [geograph-4389975]; p. 26 © Jon Yates & the Revd
Margaret King; p. 27 (*St Ethelbert's, Leominster*) © Tim Bridges; p. 27 (*Littledean*) © Cathy
Smith Miller; p. 30 (*East Ham church*) © Tim Bridges; p. 34 (*Bishop and Dean*) © Catherine
Cashmore; p. 39 (*Well Cottage*) © Andrew Talbot-Ponsonby; p. 41 © Peter Murphy.

Designed and typeset by Richard Wheeler.
Cover design by Richard Wheeler.

Printed and bound in Wales by Cambrian.

Logaston Press is committed to a sustainable future for our business, our readers and our
planet. This book is made from paper certified by the Forest Stewardship Council.

FSC
www.fsc.org
MIX
Paper from
responsible sources
FSC® C005094

British Library Catalogue in Publishing Data.
A CIP catalogue record for this book is available from the British Library.

PREFACE

HEREFORD IS UNIQUE among English Cathedrals in having a dedication to St Ethelbert the King – an obscure figure from Anglo-Saxon times, yet one who has given his name not only to our Cathedral but also to many aspects of Hereford's city and community.

This introduction contains a pictorial guide to the chief aspects of Ethelbert's life and history – it is hoped this will enable a better understanding of this little-known figure. Also included is a more detailed account of the Saint, originally written in 1994 (for the 1200th anniversary of Ethelbert's death in 794) by Meryl Jancey, then honorary archivist at Hereford Cathedral. This section has been revised and updated by Ian Bass and Lydia Prosser, and I am grateful to them for their help and support in this. With its improved footnotes, this section gives the reader the opportunity to look at original texts and takes into account more recent discoveries which throw new light on the Saint's life and background.

Part of the impetus for this booklet comes from the formation of the Order of St Ethelbert in 2015. The Order is a company of men and women, honoured by the bishop for their contribution to the life and work of the diocese, and it is hoped that the establishment of this group of people will be further incentive to learn more about our Saint.

St Ethelbert plays an important part in the life and worship of the Cathedral and so there is an appendix with prayers and other devotions which it is hoped will prove useful.

Finally, a 'fun' section – a trail and quiz around Hereford Cathedral in search of as many references to Ethelbert as we can find!

I hope that, through this booklet, Ethelbert may become a little more 'real' to our generation and that his story of courage and healing may find a valued place in the life of our Cathedral, diocese and the wider church.

Michael Tavinor
Dean of Hereford
Feast of St Ethelbert, May 2018

ACKNOWLEDGEMENTS

GRATEFUL THANKS TO Ian Bass and to Lydia Prosser for their work in updating Meryl Jancey's 1994 text and for their enthusiasm for this project. This book has been made possible through the generous support of the Bishop of Hereford, the Right Revd Richard Frith, the Friends of Hereford Cathedral, and June and Leonard Chase. Canon Sandy Elliott has given valuable assistance in questions of layout, and Gordon Taylor has been unfailing in his help and support in sourcing images of St Ethelbert. In sourcing images of churches dedicated to St Ethelbert in East Anglia, I'm indebted to Simon Knott and Peter Stephens for Norfolk and Suffolk images, and Jon Yates and the Revd Margaret King for images of the Ethelbert dedication in Essex. As always, I'm grateful for the admin support I receive for projects like this from Julie Anscomb and Gill Atkins. Karen and Andy Johnson have given wise guidance in respect of the book's publication – guidance which has been continued by Richard and Su Wheeler, now directing Logaston Press and who have seen the book to publication.

St Ethelbert, as depicted in the west window by Hardman at Belmont Abbey

INTRODUCTION

THE TRADITIONAL STORY of King Ethelbert II of East Anglia, royal saint and martyr, is soon told. In the last decade of the eighth century, the young King of the East Angles came to Offa, King of Mercia, to seek the hand of Offa's daughter in marriage. On 20 May 794, at Sutton Walls near Marden in Herefordshire, King Offa had King Ethelbert murdered. Ethelbert's mutilated body and severed head were thrown into marshes next to the River Lugg. A column of light revealed where the body and head were, and a miraculous spring appeared. This formed the location for Marden church which was originally dedicated to St Ethelbert, and the well can still be seen in the vestry today. After appearing in a vision to a nobleman, Ethelbert's body was later discovered and buried at the site of the Saxon minster at Hereford where a miraculous cult developed at his shrine.

Recounted in this way, the events seem far away, and its actors dim figures of little relevance to us in the modern day, but an examination of the way in which this story survived brings its significance to mind. By tracing this story, we begin to understand more of this young king – one in the long line of royal Saxon saints in whose life and death later ages found cause for the veneration of goodness victimised and innocence vindicated.

The traditional shield of St Ethelbert (Lady Chapel reredos)

THE STORY OF ETHELBERT

The birth of Ethelbert to Leofruna his mother and Athelred his father

Ethelbert is crowned King of the East Angles at the age of fourteen

Ethelbert sets out for Mercia. The sun is darkened. There is an earthquake

A singer sings of his royal lineage. Ethelbert gives him a bracelet

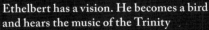

Ethelbert has a vision. He becomes a bird and hears the music of the Trinity

Ethelbert is spotted from a window by his would-be wife, Alfrytha

King Offa's queen gives false rumour that Ethelbert is come with hostile intent

Ethelbert is seized, beheaded and gains a martyr's crown, 20 May 794

3

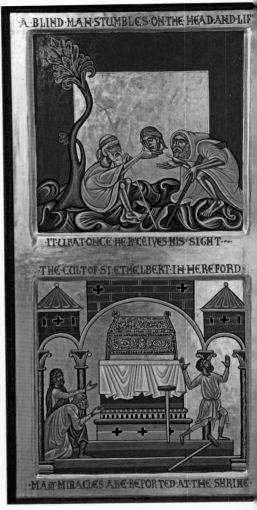

Ethelbert's body is thrown into the River Lugg. A column of light shines. A spring rises at Marden

Ethelbert's body is found and taken by ox-cart to Hereford. At Lyde the head falls from the cart

A blind man stumbles on the head and lifts it up. At once he receives his sight

Ethelbert is proclaimed a saint and his shrine at Hereford becomes a place of miraculous healing

EARLY IMAGES & REFERENCES TO ETHELBERT

THE CULT OF St Ethelbert gave impetus to the religious life of Hereford Cathedral and may account for the extension of the Cathedral eastwards in the early thirteenth century – an improved setting for the tomb/ shrine, being promoted in the late twelfth century by the *Life* written by Gerald of Wales and by the quest for new relics of the saint.

In 1055, Gruffudd ap Llywelyn sacked Hereford. Three canons were killed in the attack and the relics of Ethelbert were destroyed. The saint's head, however, appears to have survived and passed into the possession of Westminster Abbey, where it remained until the Dissolution during the 1530s.

Ethelbert's influence survived in Hereford – his feast, 20 May, the starting date of Hereford's major annual fair, was also the term day for payment of peppercorn rents.

However, the lack of relics meant that it was hard to make the cult attractive to pilgrims, although a tooth reputed to be that of Ethelbert was obtained by the community in 1228 and became a focus of devotion. Hereford, until the growth of the Cantilupe cult at the end of the thirteenth century, was at a disadvantage compared with neighbouring Worcester with its cult of Wulfstan.

Coins bearing the image of Ethelbert
Four coins of the late eighth century minted during the short reign of Ethelbert survive. One of these was discovered in 2014 in a Sussex field – an Anglo-Saxon silver penny with the name of King Ethelbert engraved on it. Some believe that the coin may have led to Ethelbert's beheading by Offa, as it had been struck as a sign of political independence.

Right: fifteenth-century statue
Richard Mayew (Bishop of Hereford 1504–16)
left instructions in his will that he wished to be
buried 'near the effigy of the holy and glorious
Ethelbert, king and martyr'. His wish was
carried out and his tomb is on the south side
of the High Altar, close to the now defaced
Ethelbert effigy. The fourteenth-century statue
was rediscovered in *c*.1727, when it was thought
to represent Richard II. It was restored to its
probable original position in *c*.1840.

Above: brass on Cantilupe shrine (*c*.1287)
Hereford Cathedral once had a wealth of
monumental brasses, of which many have
perished. The brass to Ethelbert remains. It
was originally placed within the shrine of St
Thomas of Hereford, reminding all of the close
link between the two saints. Ethelbert is shown
seated, holding his severed head. It appears
to have been produced by the London-based
Ashford workshop and is one of the earliest
brasses made in England. It is no longer kept in
the Cathedral, but its original indent can still be
seen in the Cantilupe shrine.

Fifteenth-century stained glass

St Ethelbert may be seen in stained glass in the south choir aisle. This dates from the fourteenth century and was only discovered during the extensive restoration of the Cathedral in the mid nineteenth century, when all the windows were given much needed attention. William Warrington (1796–1869) was engaged to install new glass in three windows, and during the course of his work, he discovered several boxes containing fourteenth-century glass, and restored this to its proper location. St Ethelbert takes his place alongside St Mary Magdalene, St Augustine and St George.

S:ETHELBERTVS

Left: the Ethelbert Cross

In 1841, during restoration of the Cathedral, the heads of two crosses were discovered. The finest is English and dates from the fifteenth century – intended both for use on the altar and for processions. The four symbols of the Evangelists appear in the roundels at the ends of the arms of the cross. The cross has no particular original connection with Ethelbert, but in 1976 as part of the 300th anniversary of the diocese, the cross was chosen to lead the Pilgrimage of Prayer throughout the diocese. In 1994 it was again revived as the 'Ethelbert Cross' for the celebration of the 1200th anniversary of the martyrdom of the Cathedral's patron saint.

Right: brass depicting Precentor Porter

Many Hereford clergy were commemorated by monumental brasses. Among those which have survived is one to Precentor William Porter (1524), which shows a fine Annunciation scene, and has Ethelbert holding the Cathedral and appearing as an old man. Thus, centuries after the life and death of Ethelbert, when there was no remaining physical presence to the Saint in the Cathedral, clergy still wished to be associated with their Saint.

Opposite: tomb of Peter, Lord Grandisson (d.1358) Grandisson's image, with its 1350s-style armour, and restored imagery of the saints of Hereford above, from left to right: Thomas Cantilupe, Ethelbert, John the Baptist, Thomas Becket, flanking the Coronation of the Virgin. The tomb occupies an important position opposite the newly established shrine of St Thomas, whose relics were translated here in 1349, the year of the Black Death.

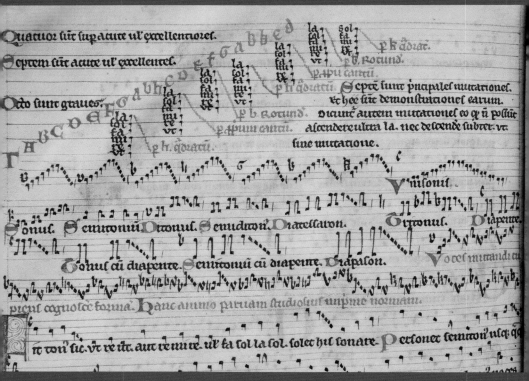

Music for Ethelbert in the *Use of Hereford*

While most of England followed the so-called *Sarum Use* in liturgy – the rite originating in the Cathedral at Salisbury – Hereford followed its own *Use*, which differed from *Sarum* in important details. Some of these details appear to have originated in France, brought to Hereford by successive bishops, including from Rouen by Bishop Gerard (1096–1100). Much of what we know about the *Use of Hereford* is derived from the magnificent noted breviary – a unique testimony to the music and text of the *Use of Hereford* in the thirteenth century.

Some chants – those in the *Temporale* – appear to be unique to Hereford. These occur mainly in the office for St Ethelbert, in which the canticle-antiphons for lauds and vespers are especially beautiful. Here we see an extract for Mattins on the Feast of St Ethelbert – the text of the second lesson ('Cum de morte …') is preceded by the end of the responsory 'illustris regis …'

ST ETHELBERT'S HOSPITAL

I N ABOUT 1225, during the episcopacy of Hugh Foliot, Elias of Bristol, a canon of Hereford, founded 'a house for the poor', said to be 'next to the cemetery of St Ethelbert's.' The hospital was welcomed by the citizens of Hereford, who dedicated a tithe of the tolls from their October fair for its support. It was placed under the authority of the Dean and Chapter, and when, in 1252, Bishop Peter Aigueblanche fell out with them, they were accused of neglecting to provide daily food for one hundred paupers at the hospital – a huge number of inmates! The hospital was located in the north-west corner of the present Cathedral Close from 1225 to the mid sixteenth century, when it moved from Broad Street to Castle Street, occupying a series of cottages beneath the castle ramparts. The statutes of 1583 insisted that the Master should be a resident canon. His income was to be derived from the fines payable on the renewal of leases. The dean was to visit the hospital every year. Contemporary documents suggest that there were nine inmates in 1588 (five men and four women), while by 1590 there were two men and eight women. Although men were never officially excluded, by the eighteenth century St Ethelbert's was almost exclusively devoted to the relief of poor women. The inmates were chosen by the dean and the master and had to be 'of venerable age and agreeable manners', and 'to conduct themselves well'. The statutes state

that, 'Notwithstanding the present shortage of means', the inmates were to receive a loaf of bread 'free of bran and well baked' weighing half a pound every day. This was supplied from the canons' bakery at a cost of £6 10s. per year. On Sunday a penny was given with the bread, but if an inmate failed to attend daily morning and evening prayers

at the Cathedral the penny and bread were withheld. These requirements were repeated almost verbatim in the Laudian statutes of 1636.

The almshouses were completely rebuilt in 1805 following a visitation by the Dean, who found them in a 'ruinous state'. The masons used stone from a local quarry and incorporated mouldings and medieval sculpture from the ruined Chapter House, giving the building a picturesque and antique quality. The seal of St Ethelbert, carved in Painswick stone, was set up over the door of the hospital. A well was also dug in the garden and a Royal George peach from Kings Acre Nursery was planted and trained along the south wall of the building. Contemporaries agreed that the end result was 'very appropriate and pleasing' and the hospital added a picturesque touch to Castle Green, which was a favourite resort for the citizens of Hereford during this era. Unlike many almshouses of the period, St Ethelbert's was clearly a well-run establishment. In the 1830s the Charity Commissioners spoke of 'an air of cheerfulness and cleanliness which clearly shows that a proper and judicious superintendence has been exercised by those who have management of its affairs.'

In recent years there have been successive refurbishments of the hospital and it remains an important part of the Chapter's responsibilities.

NINETEENTH-CENTURY REVIVAL OF INTEREST IN ETHELBERT

T HE NINETEENTH CENTURY saw a revival of interest in the saints. For Roman Catholics this meant an increased focus on the relics of saints, both pre- and post-Reformation. For Anglicans this meant a celebration of the saints, not as reasons for ritual devotion but as examples of faith and courage. With the rediscovery of the ministry of cathedrals, saints achieved a new prominence, and as their buildings were restored by the Victorians, so images of the saints proliferated – in glass, stone and wood. The feasts of saints were again celebrated and major anniversaries of dioceses linked to the lives of patron saints.

Roundel in chancel pavement
As part of the 1860's restoration of the chancel, a roundel was placed in front of the High Altar, depicting the beheading of Ethelbert. It is part of the tile ensemble provided by Messrs Godwin of Lugwardine.

Statue over High Altar
The arch at the eastern end of the chancel is surmounted by a statue of Ethelbert by N.J. Cottingham, 1852.

Statue at west end of Precentor's stall
This statue, together with that of the Blessed Virgin Mary, adjacent to the Dean's stall, was placed here in 1915 in memory of Frances Turner Atlay, widow of Bishop James Atlay, Bishop of Hereford, 1868–95.

Statue on inner porch
The inner north porch was completed in
1925 as a memorial to Dean James Leigh.
It has a statue of Ethelbert – seen not as a
young man, which he almost certainly was,
but as a mature warrior.

Statue in Lady Chapel reredos
Ethelbert appears as a Saxon warrior.
Reredos by K. Randoll Blacking (1952)

Roundel on west end wall
Wyatt's late eighteenth-century west end was replaced in stages. In 1902–08, John Oldrid
Scott designed a roundel above the side porch depicting the murder of Ethelbert, carved by
Baker & Fincher.

Stained glass in south transept
The stained glass window in the south wall of the south transept is by the firm of C.E. Kempe. It dates from 1895 and is Kempe's largest single window. It commemorates George Herbert, Dean 1868–93, and represents a text from *Te deum laudamus*: 'the glorious company of the apostles praise thee'. Pevsner called it 'pedestrian and parochial' but it is particularly interesting in its depiction of local saints – St Thomas of Hereford, St Dubricius and St Ethelbert.

ST ETHELBERT OUTSIDE HEREFORD

E THELBERT WAS A native of East Anglia, with Hereford the place of his death and subsequent cult. Apart from the Cathedral, there are no ancient churches dedicated to him in Hereford, but in East Anglia there are no less than twelve:

CHURCHES IN NORFOLK

Above: LARLING A church with a Perpendicular west tower for which bequests were made in 1473–94, the first for 'ad fabrica nova campanilis'. It was restored in 1889 for £230.

Opposite, clockwise from top left: THURTON A thatched church of the early fourteenth century. THURTON Inside, a great deal of stained glass from the sixteenth to the eighteenth century survives, including a fine 'Eucharistia'. EAST WRETHAM A church of 1865, designed by G.E. Street. BURNHAM SUTTON The parish was amalgamated with Burnham Ulph in 1422 and the church was demolished in 1771, leaving only fragments. MUNDHAM A church almost impossible to see during the summer! It was made redundant in 1749 but well into the nineteenth century it was possible for antiquarians to date it as largely thirteenth/ fourteenth-century. ALBY There are numerous bequests to the building of the tower 1497–1518, including one in 1503 for '10 chalders of lime for the tower' – an enormous amount, about 500 bushels!

ST ETHELBERT'S GATE, NORWICH The earliest surviving gate to the Cathedral, dating from the first half of the fourteenth century. According to tradition, the townsfolk broke down the original gate during the riot of 1272 and rebuilt the new gate in honour of St Ethelbert as a penance. The gate's second storey is used as a chapel in the Saint's memory.

Above and left: HERRINGSWELL A church rebuilt by A.W. Blomfield 1869–70, and with early twentieth-century stained glass by Christopher Whall and James Clark.

Below: FALKENHAM The church is of 1806, with gothic detail added later in the nineteenth century.

TANNINGTON The chancel is of *c.*1300. Inside the church is a fine series of benches with poppy heads, including a number showing the Sacraments.

Above and opposite: HESSETT A church entirely Perpendicular in style, much of it built with money from John Hoo, a wealthy merchant. There are fine wall paintings, including one of the Seven Deadly Sins, with a tree growing out of the Mouth of Hell.

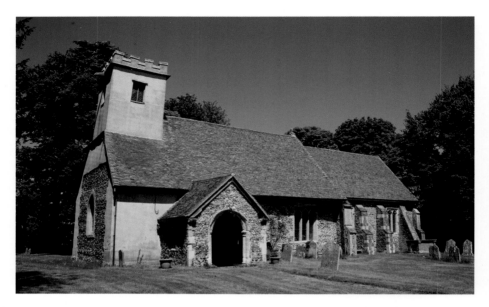

BELCHAMP OTTEN, ESSEX A Norman nave with a thirteenth- or fourteenth-century chancel. Inside, early nineteenth-century box pews and a tiny north-west gallery.

Above and right: ST ETHELBERT'S ROMAN CATHOLIC CHURCH, LEOMINSTER Designed by P.P. Pugin, 1887–88. The interior has a memorial tablet by Eric Gill.

Below: LITTLEDEAN, GLOUCESTERSHIRE With its dedication, a reminder that this part of Gloucestershire (The Forest of Dean) was in the diocese of Hereford until the Reformation. The fourteenth-century tower originally had a spire, but this was destroyed by a gale in 1894.

MARDEN CHURCH – ETHELBERT'S WELL
The well is now dry but it fills with water when the nearby River Lugg floods. The octagonal balustrade is early twentieth-century. The well had a reputation for the healing of eye diseases.

MARDEN CHURCH
The site of St Mary's church is said to be that of the first burial place of King Ethelbert, after his murder while visiting King Offa's palace nearby. The church is now substantially fourteenth-century but there are sections rebuilt by Thomas Nicholson, 1858–60.

St Albans Abbey According to the account of Matthew Paris, a thirteenth-century monk of St Albans, his Abbey was founded by Offa II, king of the Mercians, in atonement for the murder of Ethelbert. The nave reredos with its seven new statues is by Rory Young.

St George and St Ethelbert, East Ham During the 1930s, the bishop of Chelmsford appealed for support from the wider church to establish new church buildings in the populous East London part of his diocese. This caught the imagination of the rural diocese of Hereford and there was a considerable fund-raising initiative, spearheaded by the then bishop, Charles Lisle-Carr. Residents of county and diocese gave cash gifts and jewellery and raised well over £11,000 – the greater part of the cost of the church. Bishop Lisle Carr laid the foundation stone of the new church in 1935 and the design – by Newberry and Fowler – loosely resembles that of Hereford Cathedral, with its central tower. Although originally dedicated to St George, when the church was consecrated, its patron saints became 'St George and St Ethelbert', as a means of paying honour to Hereford.

Visit of congregation of Hereford Cathedral to St George and St Ethelbert, East Ham, October 2012 – the 70th anniversary of the Consecration of the church.

ST ETHELBERT IN CATHEDRAL LIFE TODAY

ALTHOUGH A LESSER-known saint in England, St Ethelbert occupies an honoured place in the community at Hereford. His story, though surrounded with medieval legend, is a moving one and has important things to say today – about courage, goodness, corruption in high places, youth and healing.

In recent years there has been a resurgence in interest in St Ethelbert as Hereford Cathedral's Saxon patron saint, with additions to the Cathedral fabric, together with the development of commemorations and events associated with the Saint.

St Ethelbert's Well The restored well on Castle Green no longer produces natural water, but each year, on the Feast of St Ethelbert, water is 'engineered' to issue from the well. The well itself is decorated with flowers and the congregation gathers there for 'sprinkling' before processing to the Cathedral for the Eucharist.

St Ethelbert's Day
As part of celebrations surrounding the dedication of the refurbished Cathedral Close, a huge papier mâché statue of Ethelbert was created and carried in liturgical celebrations. Here we see the celebration on St Ethelbert's day, 2012.

The annual St Ethelbert lecture On or about 20 May, Ethelbert is celebrated by the community. There is an annual lecture at which scholars speak on aspects of Hereford's history, including the life and legacy of Ethelbert.

Pilgrims taking part in an Ethelbert pilgrimage arrive at Hereford Cathedral

The Order of St Ethelbert

The Order of St Ethelbert was instituted in 2015. This is to honour men and women from the diocese who have contributed to the life and ministry of their communities – often over many years. About 20–25 are honoured each year at a ceremony in the Cathedral, during which the bishop presents each recipient with a certificate and a medal, featuring the three crowns of the arms of St Ethelbert (above).

The May Fair This takes place each May and is often known as St Ethelbert's Fair. Until 1838 its rights were vested in the Bishop of Hereford. A local Act of Parliament at that time transferred the rights to the Council and reduced the length of the fair's duration as, 'it would greatly tend to the advantage of the City and to the improvement of the morals of the inhabitants thereof.' For the privilege of holding the fair, the 1838 Act provides that the Council pay twelve and a half bushels of the best wheat, or the equivalent in monetary terms, annually to the Bishop of Hereford. While this payment was formally commuted in 1971, the fair is still opened with the colourful and traditional ceremony of weighing the wheat.

Following the opening of the fair, the Bishop traditionally joins the mayor and councillors in enjoying rides on the various attractions. Here we see Dean and Bishop on the 'wheel' at the May Fair opening in May 2017. The photograph was submitted to the *Church Times* for their weekly caption competition and became the winning entry with its caption: 'Mick and Rick, being sick' – a reference to Bishop Richard and Dean Michael!

The visit of HM The Queen with St Ethelbert in attendance! On 12 July 2012, HM The Queen visited Hereford, as part of her 'Diamond Day' visits to various parts of the country. As she met the people of Hereford in the Cathedral Close, an earlier resident of Hereford – Ethelbert the King – was in the background, towering over the scene!

Above: **Shrine of St Ethelbert (2007)** Peter Murphy working on icons.

Opposite: The shrine of St Ethelbert (2007) Although Ethelbert's image appears in many places in the Cathedral, there had never been a modern 'focus' of prayer. In 2007, a new shrine-like structure was created, on the presumed site of the original shrine, east of the High Altar. Designed by Robert Kilgour, it was made by Stephen Florence and decorated with icon-images by Peter Murphy. The shrine provides a focus for processions on the feast of St Ethelbert and introduces to this area of the Cathedral bright and vivid colour, such as would have been common in medieval times. Round the shrine are carved words of Jesus: *All who want to be followers of mine must renounce self. Day after day they must take up their cross and follow me.* (Luke 9.23)

Right: St Ethelbert roundel in Cathedral Close (2011) The Cathedral Close was refurbished in 2009–11 and a series of metal roundels inserted in the ground, depicting various aspects of the Cathedral's history.

St Ethelbert's Well The earliest reference to a well dedicated to the Saint occurs in a document referring to a grant of land to the Dean and Chapter in 1250. The land is said to lie towards the 'fontem beati Ethelberti', in the castle precincts. With the decline of the castle in the fourteenth century, Bishop Swinfield constructed a stone canopy over the well to assist pilgrims coming to Hereford to visit the shrine – not of Ethelbert but of St Thomas Cantilupe. The structure seems to have been still in place in 1610, when it appears on Speed's plan, and again in 1684, when it was sketched by Dinely (**above**), and finally in 1721, sketched by Stukeley (**right**), but subsequent references are scarce. In 1780, the Improvement Commissioners connected the culverts from Castle Street into 'the drain leading from St Ethelbert's Well to the river'.

By the nineteenth century, the well was still in place and was visited by 'persons afflicted by ulcers and sores of various kinds', but it seems to have been reconstructed at that time, incorporating a crowned head of St Ethelbert, removed from the west front of the Cathedral and protected by an iron grille. In 1822 the water was analysed by Mr J. Murray who found that it had a stable temperature of 52 degrees and contained some 'super carbonate of lime, muriate of magnesia and alum', but he concluded that the water was not especially medicinal.

As late as the 1860s, the *Hereford Times* recorded that 'a number of old inhabitants of the City still go down at early morn to quaff a draught of the water to cure weak eyes'. From 1830, the water was used to provide bathing in the area beneath the Castle Green Reading Room, and there was even talk of bottling the water – an idea that was quickly abandoned as the water was found to be badly polluted by seepage from the city sewers. The remains of the well may still be seen in the garden of Well Cottage (**above**). The present cast-iron drinking fountain, in the niche on Castle Green (**right**), dates from 1904 and the whole structure was rededicated by Bishop John Eastaugh on St Ethelbert's Day, 20 May 1978.

Hereford Cathedral School

Throughout much of its history, Hereford Cathedral has been responsible for the education of the young, not least through its own Cathedral School, which can trace its origins back to the fourteenth century. The school gathers daily for prayers in the Cathedral and, during services, the school mace is carried. Above the school crest, the letters of the school motto form a balustrade, which is surmounted by a three-dimensional image of St Ethelbert holding his head in his hands. The mace was made by Alan Johansson and dedicated in March 1983 to the memory of Major Michel Forge of the Royal Corps of Signals, who died on 6 June 1982, the one Old Herefordian fatality of the Falklands War.

St Ethelbert among the saints of Hereford St Ethelbert is just one of Hereford's saints –
saints which nurture the life and worship of the Cathedral throughout the year. In this icon
by Peter Murphy we see, left to right: Ethelbert, Thomas of Hereford, The Blessed Virgin
Mary with Our Lord, Thomas Traherne, and St John the Baptist.

A Prayer

Almighty God, by whose grace and power your holy martyr Ethelbert triumphed over suffering and was faithful unto death: Strengthen us by your grace, that we may endure reproach and persecution, and faithfully bear witness to the name of Jesus Christ our Lord. **Amen.**

Collect

O God, the founder and governor of all earthly kingdoms, who gives us this holy day to recall the mortal anguish of the blessed king and martyr, your servant Ethelbert: grant that as we rejoice to remember him on earth, so may we be one with him in the communion of your saints in heaven; through Jesus Christ our Lord.

A Pilgrimage for Today – Ethelbert and our Prayers

HEREFORD CATHEDRAL IS dedicated to the Blessed Virgin Mary and St Ethelbert the King – not to be confused with Canterbury's St Ethelbert, the first Anglo-Saxon king. Hereford's Ethelbert was born in East Anglia in the late eighth century. He journeyed to Mercia to seek the hand of Aelfrytha, daughter of King Offa. For political reasons, Offa had the young king murdered – traditionally on 20 May 794 – at Marden, five miles from Hereford.

The shrine of St Ethelbert tells the story of the Saint's life in thirteen panels, painted by Peter Murphy. It was designed by the Cathedral Architect, Robert Kilgour and made by Stephen Florence. It may well be near the site of the burial place of Ethelbert – and certainly, the shrine of a cathedral's saint was often in this position, east of the High Altar. All are invited to use this prayer guide – helping us to find relevance today in this story from the eighth century.

IMAGE ONE   The Birth of Ethelbert

We give thanks for our early life – for parents – for teachers – for all who cared for us and influenced us in our early years. Have we been baptized? We pray for strength to fulfil our promises.

IMAGE TWO   Ethelbert is crowned king of the East Angles at the age of fourteen

Pray for all who bear the weight of authority – in Church and State. We remember our own responsibilities – in our families – in our work. We pray for all leaders that they may work with justice and integrity. We pray for all young people for whom we care – our children, grandchildren and godchildren. We pray for young people who have great responsibility thrust upon them at an early age.

IMAGE THREE Ethelbert sets out for Mercia from Bury St Edmunds. The sun is darkened and there is an earthquake

In our world, many lives are terribly affected by natural disaster. Many are still rebuilding their communities after recent tsunamis and earthquakes. We pray for all relief organisations. We pray for generosity to respond to those in need. Ethelbert saw meaning in the natural world. We pray that we may have spirits open to all that is round us.

IMAGE FOUR A singer sings of his royal lineage. Ethelbert gives him a bracelet

Music is so often an important part of our lives. We remember all who make music in this Cathedral church. Ethelbert received an object of beauty – we give thanks for material things which are important to us – and pray for generosity in our sharing of them.

IMAGE FIVE Ethelbert has a vision on the journey

We give thanks for times when we've been able to pray – we remember times when it has been really hard to pray. We give thanks for this Cathedral as a place of prayer – a place where many leave their prayers at the Shrine of St Thomas. Might we leave a prayer here today?

IMAGE SIX Ethelbert is spotted by his wife-to-be, Aelfrytha

We remember those close to us – spouse, partner, family and friends. We give thanks for the care and support we rely on. We pray, too, for those we find it hard to love – for those we find difficult.

IMAGE SEVEN **Ethelbert is victim of a whispering campaign**

We pray for an end to all forms of discrimination in our society – discrimination on the grounds of colour, religion, race, sexuality, gender, politics, lifestyle. We pray for an openness to humanity in all its rich variety.

IMAGE EIGHT **Ethelbert is beheaded**

We remember all who suffer under harsh and cruel regimes – all unjustly in prison. We remember prisoners of conscience and the work of Amnesty International. We remember societies where there is still capital punishment.

IMAGE NINE **Ethelbert's body is thrown into the river. A light shines, a spring rises**

We give thanks for times when we have known light shining after a period of darkness in our lives – when we have been helped through bereavement, depression or anxiety – by the help and support of others.

IMAGE TEN **Ethelbert's body is taken by ox-cart to Hereford. The head falls from the cart**

Animals play their part in the story. We pray for the animal world – for justice and for care – for an end to exploitation. We remember the part animals play in our own lives and pray for all who care for them.

IMAGE ELEVEN A blind man stumbles on the head and retrieves it. He receives sight

We remember all in need and all who seek to help them. In our community of Hereford we pray for our local hospitals – we pray for the work of the Royal National College for the Blind.

IMAGE TWELVE Many pilgrims come to the shrine and find healing

We pray for the work of this Cathedral – as a place of Christian worship and pilgrimage – as a building of history and beauty – as a focus for county and city – as the seat of the Bishop – as mother Church of the diocese of Hereford.

IMAGE THIRTEEN Ethelbert, King and Martyr – pray for us

We give thanks for the saints. We remember saints we have known in our own lives – all who have, by their kindness and example, given us glimpses of God. We pray for those we love but see no longer – that they may rest in the peace of Christ.

Words round the Shrine

Jesus said: All who want to be followers of mine must renounce self. Day after day they must take up their cross and follow me. (Luke 9.23)

St Ethelbert Quiz*

H EREFORD'S PATRON SAINT, St Ethelbert, King and Martyr may not be the most well-known saint in England but his story has shaped Hereford's history, and today, more than 1200 years after his life and death, he is remembered in many ways in our community:

St Ethelbert's Well, on Castle Green
St Ethelbert Street
St Ethelbert House
St Ethelbert's Hospital Almshouses
St Ethelbert's Fair, or the May Fair,
held each year

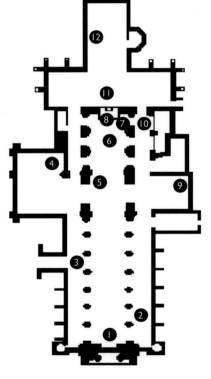

While there are at least ten churches dedicated to St Ethelbert in East Anglia, there are, surprisingly, none in this part of the world – except for the Catholic church in Leominster and, of course, the Cathedral, where Ethelbert's name lives on in his annual celebration.

There are a large number of images of Ethelbert in the Cathedral itself, but they are often quite difficult to identify – see if you can! The clues below will lead you to them, and the map of the Cathedral will show you the location of the image. Remember to look up as well as down! Do consult the modern notices near to the numbered locations – these will help you identify the spot and image. Good luck!

Find the places shown on the map. Each has an image of St Ethelbert.

1. Which female monarch is at the bottom of the window in which Ethelbert is portrayed?

   ....

2. What year was this image of Ethelbert woven?

   ....

3. What does Ethelbert hold in his right hand?

   ....

4. Ethelbert is portrayed in the border of the brass to Dean ...?

   ....

5. A wooden Ethelbert is facing west from whose stall?

   ....

6. Roman numerals suggest a discrepancy in the date of Ethelbert's death. Or do they?

   ....

7. From which century does this famous (and defaced) statue of Ethelbert date?

   ....

8. How would you describe the demeanour of the angel sitting beneath the standing Ethelbert?

   ....

9. Name a saint to the right or left of, or below, Ethelbert in this window?

   ....

10. Name a saint to the right or left of Ethelbert in this window?

    ....

11. What Biblical text is associated with Ethelbert's modern shrine?

    ....

12. Above whose tomb is there a statue of Ethelbert?

    ....

*Answers on page 60

St Ethelbert
Patron Saint of Hereford Cathedral

First Edition by E.M. Jancey MA, Honorary Archivist, Hereford Cathedral (1994)
Revised by Ian Bass and Lydia Prosser (2017 & 2018)

T HE EARLIEST ACCOUNT of the death of Ethelbert is given in the *Anglo-Saxon Chronicles*.[1] The *Chronicles*, which date from the ninth century but incorporate much older material, are a series of annals copied in monasteries across the country and added to annually with the recording of the important ecclesiastical and political events of that year. The entry for the death of St Ethelbert is stark indeed. Under the year 794 is given:

> *Her Offa Miercna cyning het Epelbryhte rex pæt heafod ofaslean.*
> 'This year Offa, king of the Mercians, commanded the head of King Ethelbert to be struck off.'[2]

While nothing is related of the events that led up to, and followed, this extreme action and no motive is suggested, the annal entry is a tantalising precis of a story that captured the imagination, spawning many fuller versions in the twelfth century that added the necessary missing information. Some of these later versions may even be taken from traditions remembered from the time of the murder, although the extent is impossible to judge.

John of Worcester, who was probably a monk of the Benedictine abbey there, compiled a chronicle history in the early twelfth century which adds a little to the *Anglo-Saxon Chronicle's* entry concerning Ethelbert.[3] He says that King Offa was prompted to do this deed by the wicked incitement of his queen, Cynethryth. We know that Cynethryth was a highly prominent figure in the Mercian court: she is the only queen of Anglo-Saxon England who is known to have had coins minted in her own name. Politics was a dangerous business in this period and it is intriguing that another contemporary female of the family of Offa is known to have indulged in murder. The monk Asser, in his *Life of*

King Alfred, relates how one of the daughters of Cynethryth and Offa – a certain Eadburgh – was accustomed to poison people, including, accidentally, her own husband, the King of Wessex.[4] Cynethryth herself has been linked with the murderous wife of the Offa mentioned in the epic old English poem *Beowulf*, who arranged the murders of any noblemen to whom she took a dislike, before she was reformed through marriage to Offa.[5]

William of Malmesbury, a historian writing a little later in the twelfth century, presents a picture of Offa as a king in whom virtue and vice were strangely mixed. He tells how Offa beheaded Ethelbert in an act of perfidy, betraying one who had come deluded by promises:

> When I think of his achievements, I am in doubt whether to praise or to condemn; to such an extent did vices at one moment cloak themselves with virtues, and virtue at another take the place of vice, in one and the same man [...] When he thought treachery more likely to be profitable, he invited King Æthelberht to visit him, attracting him with handsome promises; once within his palace walls, he lulled his suspicions with spurious affability, and suddenly had him beheaded, after which he overran without any right the kingdom of the East Angles, which Æthelberht had held.[6]

The contemporary sources concerned with Offa give a similarly mixed view of him. Offa was undoubtedly the most powerful king of his day. His kingdom stretched beyond Mercia, covering Sussex, Kent, East Anglia and the kingdom of the *Hwicce* directly, as well as indirectly through marriage ties with the ruling families of Northumbria and Wessex. He corresponded with the great king Charlemagne and was praised by Alcuin, a Northumbrian scholar based at the court of Charlemagne, for his piety and interest in learning. Yet, Alcuin also refers in his letters to the bloodthirsty killing that attended Offa's reign, remarking that the early death of Offa's son Ecgfrith was brought about 'not for his own sins, but the vengeance for the blood shed by the father has reached the son. For you know very well how much blood his father shed to secure the kingdom on his son.'[7] William of Malmesbury's account not only reflects the contemporary shock that such a man could commit such atrocities, but also responds to the horror of events that were happening parallel to this within a neighbouring kingdom. In 796, just two years after the murder of King Ethelbert, the King of Northumbria, Ethelred, was brutally murdered by his own people.[8] It seems that treachery was in the air. Another letter of Alcuin records the reaction of Charlemagne to this calamity: 'greatly enraged against that nation, [he] held "that perfidious and perverse race, murderers of their lords", as he called them, worse than pagans.'[9] We can only imagine that a similar reaction would have been provoked by the murder of Ethelbert in 794 and perhaps this letter, which is addressed to Offa, may have been intended as a subtle remonstrance to the Mercian king. A preoccupation with treachery and the horror of violence between individuals bound by hospitality are common themes in the literature of the Anglo-Saxon period.[10] These themes have universal appeal, particularly in a world where order was created and defined by rank and prescribed codes of behaviour.

The story of Ethelbert was further remembered and expounded for another reason. John of Worcester speaks of him as a martyr. This term does not necessarily describe one who dies at the hands of pagans for their faith, but can also refer to one dying as the innocent victim of evil. John of Worcester celebrates 'the most glorious and most holy Æthelberht, king of the East Angles, pleasing to Christ by reason of his virtues, gracious to all with his agreeable speech [...] unrighteously slain, [who] was taken from earth by a great band of angels and entered the courts of the blessed.'[11] Mention of the cult at Hereford where Ethelbert was venerated is first made by John of Worcester. The entry for the year 1055 implies that the shrine which was the focus of this cult was rich and important. In that year the rebel Ælfgar and his Welsh allies attacked Hereford. The army entered the city, slew seven canons who defended the door of the principal church, and burned the minster which Athelstan, bishop since 1012 (and by 1055, blind) had built. According to John, the Welsh destroyed all its ornaments and the relics of St Ethelbert, king and martyr.[12]

Unlike the saints of the later Middle Ages, whose sanctity had to be proved by a vigorous and strict process, Ethelbert had become a saint by popular assent in the typical Anglo-Saxon way. His cult had grown so prominent by the end of the tenth century that the minster of St Mary at Hereford bore his name in additional dedication. In c.1000 the will of Wulfgeat of Donnington included a bequest to St Guthlac's priory and 'to St Ethelbert's [for] the equivalent of half a pound'.[13] The Normans retained the dedication to the Anglo-Saxon king, which is attested to in 1086 in the *Domesday Book*, which refers to the payments due to '*Canonicis Sancti Alberti*' (the canons of the church of St Ethelbert).

In the early twelfth century, work began on the Romanesque building which replaced Athelstan's ruined minster. It is not surprising that this renewal should have occasioned a new interest in St Ethelbert and a revival of his shrine. Indeed,

Arthur Bannister suggests that the middle of the twelfth century was the time when the real cult of St Ethelbert began, albeit somewhat hampered by the lack of relics. Unlike the cult of the Anglo-Saxon period, this cult was brought about by deliberate effort rather than popular movement.[14] The possession of relics was a matter of great importance to religious communities. They could be the focus of veneration and a point of contact to the celestial regions through which all people could come to seek healing of body and soul. The loss of these relics would be keenly felt.

Yet, the remains of St Ethelbert cannot have been completely destroyed. The severed head of St Ethelbert passed at some time – possibly even after 1055 – into the possession of Westminster Abbey. This is what probably impelled Osbert of Clare, at one time its Prior, to write a life of St Ethelbert in the mid-twelfth century.[15] The possession of relics involves the need to provide authenticity and what we might call 'provenance'. This goes some way to explain the growth of a whole class of literature: the lives of saints, written and composed as hagiography. The purpose of these lives was to induce veneration, to increase faith and to celebrate the special virtues illustrated in the life of the particular subject.[16] It is interesting that Osbert appears to have based his account on a text that survives in a manuscript of early twelfth-century date, now in Corpus Christi College, Cambridge, which seems to have originated in Hereford.[17] The following abstract gives the outline of this, the earliest full version of the Ethelbert story:[18]

King Ethelbert was descended in a long line of the royal house of the East Angles, one of his forebears was the great Redwald. His father was Athelred, his mother Leofruna. He was born in the year 779. He had a Christian upbringing. His childhood was marked by seriousness and by his desire to please Christ above all else. He succeeded his father when he was fourteen and it was suggested to him that he should think of marriage, but he demurred, wishing to remain chaste, but was persuaded that he should have an heir. The name of Syndritha, beautiful and sole heir of her father Egeon was brought forward, but he refused to contemplate wedlock with her because her father had betrayed his. Then Oswald, a counsellor, spoke of the king, Offa, his queen Kynedritha, and their daughter Alfthrytha. This suggestion was well received by all, except for Ethelbert's mother who distrusted the Mercians, and feared bad faith. But Ethelbert did not change his decision to go to Mercia.

Even as he mounted his horse, the earth shook, terrifying the whole war band. At this sign his mother feared that her son would never return.

'God's will be done', he said. But another sign followed. The sun darkened and dense mist came up so that the travellers could not see and only by calling could they know where each other was. Ethelbert, astounded by this darkening of the sun, called out to his stupefied retinue: 'let us', he said, 'kneel down and pray that Almighty God have mercy on us'. Hardly had they finished praying when all was calm. Ethelbert, in high spirits, called for godly songs to be sung, promising that a bracelet be given to the singer. And the songs that were sung told of the king's royal lineage. He was so pleased that he forthwith stripped a bracelet from his arm, promising further gifts when they returned.

And so Ethelbert came to Mercia. He lodged in the royal township of Sutton, where in the night he had a dream or vision. He seemed to see his palace in ruins and his mother coming to him weeping. Then he saw a great beam raised up, the eastern side of which dripped blood and from the south a column of light stretch to heaven. He himself was changed to a bird whose golden wings covered the beam and which flew up on high, from whence he seemed to hear sweet singing from the throne of the Trinity.

He asked of Oswald what this could mean. Oswald, after careful thought said: 'in the mercy of God, O King, whatever happens to you will be well.'

King Ethelbert made gifts to Offa,[19] but Offa gave ear to false rumour that Ethelbert was come with hostile intent to invade his kingdom.

At daylight Ethelbert hastened to Offa whose daughter Alfthrytha saw him from her solar window as he approached and ran to her mother. 'Lo', she said, 'King Ethelbert has come, a young man, outstanding, altogether splendid. He is worthy to be preferred before my father'. This praise angered her mother, who went to King Offa. She told him that there was truth in the rumour and said that if this marriage took place, Offa's kingdom would be invaded and 'he would be thrust out. Rise and do what I counsel you: promise half your kingdom to the one who will kill him'. Offa acceded to these persuasions. One Winbertus, prompted by greed at the royal promise, said to the king in secret that no one would carry out what had been suggested more easily than he. He had been a figure of some importance for fifteen years at Offa's court where he had taken refuge after having committed homicide. He, the deceitful wretch, went to meet the innocent and guileless king.

Ethelbert dismounted saying that he wished to know when he could speak with Offa. Winbertus replied that Offa knew of his coming, and had said that what he asked would be done. 'Let us go into Offa', said the blessed Ethelbert. Winbertus persuaded him to disarm, it not being fitting, in time of peace, to carry a sword in the king's presence. This, in innocence, Ethelbert did and accompanied by few nobles went into the king. The doors were shut. Ethelbert was taken, bound and beaten. Then, with his own sword he was beheaded by Winbertus.

This brings to an end the account in this version of Ethelbert's death. It then goes on to describe the effect of this death:

Offa's daughter mourned the young king, and expressing abhorrence of the wickedness of her parents vowed to give herself up to the service of God to live as an anchorite at Croyland.

The writer then goes on to balance St Ethelbert, martyr in the west, with St Edmund in the east, and brings to an end this part of the story with the statement that Ethelbert was fourteen when he died in the year 793.[20] He then begins again, with reference to the sorrows of the young king's mother and then tells how Offa ordered that Ethelbert's body be thrown into a marsh on the banks of the River Lugg. A column of light shone near the place. When Offa heard of this miracle, proving that a martyr had entered into heavenly joy, he was filled with remorse and ordered that tithes be paid throughout his kingdom. The last part of this version describes the finding of the body and tells of its eventual burial:

One Berferhtus, who had been Offa's chamberlain had a vision of the saint, who told him to seek the treasure by the River Lugg. He rose up, told a companion, Ecgmund, of the vision, by which he was commanded to find the body, place it on an ox-cart and take it to a place called Fernley near the bank of the River Wye. They found the body, the head severed, soiled with the mud of the marsh, but light shone forth from it. They washed it, wrapped it in cloths and placed it on an ox-cart, but when they reached a place called Lyde, the head fell from the cart.

Now a blind man was making his way there when his feet stumbled on an obstacle which he realised was a human head. He lifted it up and cried in an act of faith: 'O Ethelbert, whom King Offa wickedly ordered to be killed, pity me and give me sight again.' He cradled the head, and, as he had asked his sight was restored. He took the head to carry it with him, hurrying to follow the cart. He came up with it at a place called by the local people Schelwick. He cried out: 'stop, stop Bertferhtus - I have here precious treasure through which I have received my sight', and recounted what had happened.

> Bertferhtus and his companion were unaware that the head had fallen.
> At this revelation of the merits of the blessed martyr they rejoiced together,
> and the body was taken to the place designated in Bertferhtus's dream.

The writer equates this place, Fernley, as that which later became Hereford, where one Milferhtus [Milfrid] built a splendid minster. He rests his case on the fact that Ethelbert's relics were at Hereford, and ends with assurance and joy that the saint is in heaven.

This kind of material has to be approached with some care, for we are a long way from the world which is deeply familiar with literature of this kind, composed according to a convention in which the chosen subject was put in a light to reflect certain virtues, those virtues glorified by miracles. The emphasis on miracles has sometimes tended to cause serious underestimation of the value of sources such as this in their bearing on history and on the writing of history. There are, however, many indications of this version of the foundation which appear to be justified when considered alongside the picture presented by other sources.

It is quite likely that Offa had some kind of headquarters in the Sutton and Marden area at the time he completed his dyke marking the boundary with Wales. Archaeological investigation in Sutton Walls found a pit just outside of the Iron Age encampment containing the bodies of a number of males, many of which had been decapitated. These were buried above the Iron Age and Romano-British layer, placing them within an Anglo-Saxon context. Is it too much to consider that these may be the entourage of Ethelbert? [21]

Other recent archaeological discoveries have the potential to shed great light on the circumstances of Ethelbert's death. As a sub-king of a kingdom controlled by Offa, Ethelbert was limited in what he could achieve. Offa took great pains to ensure that his dominance over the rulers of subject kingdoms was publicly recognised; for example, a charter of 799 records Offa acting with great anger that Egberht, the king of Kent, had issued charters and granted land without his permission, and stripping the land from its recipient.[22] This adds potential significance to the recent discovery of no less than four coins struck under the name of Ethelbert, the latest found as recently as 2014 by a metal-detectorist in Sussex.[23] This coin has the inscription 'E ð I L B E R H · R E X'. Another coin, found in 1908 at Tivoli, Rome utilises the imperial imagery of roman coins to symbolise the sovereign power of the East Anglian Ethelbert: the one side carries an image of Romulus and Remus, the legendary founders of Rome.[24] Unfortunately, almost nothing else survives to tell us about Ethelbert's reign as king of East Anglia.

Slight evidence it may be, but these coins perhaps hint at a degree of independent power boasted by Ethelbert that may have been considered dangerous and unacceptable to Offa, and perhaps precipitated the act that followed.[25]

A later *Life*, based largely on Osbert's *Life*, was written for Hereford by *Giraldus Cambrensis* ('Gerald of Wales') around 1195.[26] A prebend at the Cathedral, Gerald produced the work at the 'insistence of [his] fellow canons'.[27] Gerald, a professional hagiographer, was famed for his style and literary flair, which was probably why he was asked to provide a polished version of the life of the patron saint.

It is an ornate piece of writing. Minor details differ from the old version, including variance in the forms of the names. A few additions are made. Gerald refers to Offa's wife as acting as Potiphar's wife did to Joseph, which adds an emphasis on the chastity of the young king as a virtue to be celebrated. He mentions the rough treatment of the severed head. He gives more details about the founding of Hereford Cathedral and of gifts made to the Church, although these read rather as legend than as history. It is, however, important to realise that in both these Hereford versions, the founding of the Cathedral and the accessions of lands to the Church are seen as the direct results of Ethelbert's martyrdom. Gerald also lists a few miracles, and promises further records of others, but they do not seem to have been written down.

Another later account with a different emphasis is the work of the historian Matthew Paris.[28] Here, Offa's queen is shown to be personally active in the murder; Offa, in his remorse, imprisoned her. Tradition has it that St Albans Abbey was founded by Offa in penance.[29] Matthew Paris was a monk of St Albans. His concern was to show the life of its founder, Offa, in the most favourable way and so the culpability of the crime is definitely directed away from Offa. This account, along with the *Life* written by Gerald of Wales, became the sources of the readings, antiphons and responses in the Offices for the saint's feast day, 20 May, in the thirteenth-century *Hereford Breviary*.[30]

The Ethelbert cult seems to have stayed active at Hereford Cathedral until well into the thirteenth century. In about 1220 it received the encouragement of the gift of the tooth as a relic, but by the end of that century it was overtaken by the new cult occasioned by the miracles at the tomb of Thomas de Cantilupe, Bishop of Hereford from 1275–82. Nonetheless, in the present day Cathedral many fragments of evidence remain to show that Ethelbert has been long remembered here. They include a brass, once inlaid on Cantilupe's tomb, a stained glass window and a beautiful stone figure of the fourteenth century, much mutilated. Ethelbert appears as a figure alongside those of SS Mary the Virgin, John the Baptist, Thomas Becket, and Thomas de Cantilupe on the tomb of Peter de Grandisson in the Lady Chapel. A well in the vicinity of the Cathedral down Quay Street, near Castle Green, still bears his name. Most recently, in 2007 a new shrine was built in the retro-choir to replace the one long destroyed and, as patron saint of the Cathedral, Ethelbert is represented on the Dean and Chapter's seal.

In the places associated with his death and the miraculous discovery of his body the tradition also lives on. The church of Marden, said to be founded on the site where his body was found, contains within its walls the well, still known as that which flowed where his head had rested and named as his. St Ethelbert has never been quite forgotten. He takes us back far into the past, a link with Anglo-Saxon England and the development of Christianity within these shores, and with the later ages which saw in his story a symbol of innocent goodness triumphant that can still resonate today.

NOTES

[1] *The Anglo-Saxon Chronicles*, ed. and trans. by Michael Swanton (London: Phoenix Press, 2000). Hereafter *ASC*.

[2] *ASC*, A recension. There has been some confusion about the date of Ethelbert's death rising from the fact that the *Anglo-Saxon Chronicle* annals from 756–828 are misplaced by two years. It is often cited as 792 or 793.

[3] John of Worcester, *The Chronicle of John of Worcester*, 2 vols., ed. and trans. R.R. Darlington, P. McGurk, and J. Bray, Oxford Medieval Texts (Oxford: Oxford University Press, 1995–98), II, p. 225.

[4] Asser, *Alfred the Great: Asser's Life of King Alfred and Other Contemporary Sources*, eds. and trans. S. Keynes and M. Lapidge (London: Penguin Group, 1983), Chapter 14, pp. 71–2.

[5] D. Whitelock, *The Audience of Beowulf* (Oxford: Clarendon Press, 1951); *Beowulf*, lines 1931b–1961.

[6] William of Malmesbury, *Gesta Regum Anglorum, The History of the English Kings*, 2 vols., ed. and trans. R.A.B. Mynors, R.M. Thomson, and M. Winterbottom, Oxford Medieval Texts (Oxford: Oxford University Press, 1998–99), I, pp. 120–3.

[7] *English Historical Documents, volume I, c.500–1042*, ed. D. Whitelock, 2nd edn. (London: Routledge, 1995), no. 202, Letter of Alcuin to Osbert (797). (Hereafter EHD).

[8] *ASC*, pp. 56–7.

[9] *EHD*, no. 198, Letter of Alcuin to Offa (796).

[10] Occurring for instance in the Finn Episode in *Beowulf*, lines 1068–1159, see also 'The Finnsburg Fragment' in *Old English Minor Heroic Poems*, ed. J. Hill (Durham: Pontifical Institute of Mediaeval Studies, 1983).

[11] John of Worcester, *Chronicle*, II, pp. 224–5.

[12] Ibid., pp. 576–9.

[13] *Anglo-Saxon Wills*, ed. and trans. D. Whitelock (Cambridge: Cambridge University Press, 1930), pp. 54–5.

[14] A.T. Bannister, *The Cathedral Church of Hereford, its History and Constitution* (London: SPCK, 1924), pp. 109–13.

[15] M.R. James, 'The Two Lives of St Ethelbert, King and Martyr', *English Historical Review*, vol. 32 (1917), pp. 214–44.

[16] S. Ridyard, *The Royal Saints of Anglo-Saxon England* (Cambridge: Cambridge University Press, 1988).

[17] James, 'The Two Lives of St Ethelbert'.

[18] Translated by E.M. Jancey 1994.

[19] Implying that he sent them before him.

[20] A comparison of the two tales is of considerable interest; both are concerned with subjects who we otherwise know very little about and the circumstances of both figures' deaths are shrouded in mystery. Both traditions include elements such as the miraculous discovery of the mutilated body of the saint. The earliest *Life of St Edmund* was produced by Abbo of Fleury, available in an edition by M. Winterbottom in his *Three Lives of English Saints* (Toronto: University of Toronto Press, 1972).

[21] K. Ray, *The Archaeology of Herefordshire: An Exploration* (Almeley: Logaston Press, 2016), pp. 219–22.

[22] *EHD*, no. 80.

[23] Available Online: <http://www.bbc.co.uk/news/uk-england-27485772> and <http://www.bbc.co.uk/news/uk-england-suffolk-27795641>

[24] I. Stewart, 'The London Mint and the Coinage of Offa' in *Anglo-Saxon Monetary History*, ed. M. Blackburn, (Leicester, 1986), pp. 31–2.

[25] M.M. Archibald and V. Fenwick, 'A Sceat of Ethelbert I of East Anglia and Recent Finds of Coins of Beonna', *British Numismatic Journal 65*, p. 13.

[26] *Giraldi Cambrensis*, *Opera*, 8 vols, eds. J.S. Brewer, F. Dimock and G.F. Warner, Rolls Series (London: Longman, Green, Longman and Roberts, 1861–91), II, p. 409; III, pp. 407–30. Also James, 'Two Lives of St Ethelbert'. See R. Bartlett, *Gerald of Wales: A Voice of the Middle Ages* (Stroud: Tempus, 1982).

[27] R. Bartlett, 'Re-writing Saints' Lives: the case of Gerald of Wales', *Speculum*, lviii (1983), pp. 598–611.

[28] Matthew Paris, *Chronica Maiora vol. I*, ed. H.R. Luard, Rolls Series (London: Longman & Co., 1872), pp. 354–5.

[29] M. Tavinor, *Shrines of the Saints in England and Wales* (Norwich: Canterbury Press, 2016), p. 9.

[30] W. Smith, *The Use of Hereford: The Sources of a Medieval English Diocesan Rite* (Farnham: Ashgate Publishing Ltd, 2015), pp. 609–15.

Seal of St Ethelbert

Answers to St Ethelbert Quiz on page 49

1. Queen Victoria
2. 1876
3. A shield
4. Dean Procester
5. The Precentor's stall
6. Roman numerals suggest AD 793; the preferred date of his death is 794
7. Fifteenth century
8. Bored!
9. St Thomas of Hereford, St David, St Augustine
10. St Mary Magdalen, St Augustine
11. 'All who want to be followers of mine must renounce self. Day after day they must take up their cross and follow me' (Luke 9.23)
12. Peter, Lord Grandisson